ECODEVIANCE

DEVIA

ECODECONFERENCE

(Soma)tics for the Future Wilderness

CAConrad

WAVE BOOKS SEATTLE AND NEW YORK

PUBLISHED BY WAVE BOOKS

WWW.WAVEPOETRY.COM

WAVE BOOKS TITLES ARE DISTRIBUTED TO THE TRADE BY

CONSORTIUM BOOK SALES AND DISTRIBUTION

PHONE: 800-283-3572 / SAN 631-760X

LIBRARY OF CONGRESS CATALOGING-IN-PUBLICATION DATA

CONRAD, C. A.

ECODEVIANCE : (SOMA)TICS FOR THE FUTURE WILDERNESS /

CACONRAD. — FIRST EDITION.

PAGES CM

ISBN 978-1-940696-00-3 (LIMITED EDITION HARDCOVER)

ISBN 978-1-940696-01-0 (TRADE PBK.)

I. TITLE.

PS3603.O555E36 2014

811'.6—DC23

2014001452

DESIGNED AND COMPOSED BY QUEMADURA

PRINTED IN THE UNITED STATES OF AMERICA

9 8 7 6 5 4 3 2

FIRST EDITION

WAVE BOOKS 046

"THIS IS A CLASSIC SLINGSHOT"

—MY GRANDMOTHER

I LOVE MY WEIRDO FRIENDS

THIS BOOK IS FOR THEM

(Soma)tic Poetry Rituals

Growing up in a rural factory town I watched my creative family extend the grind of their monotonous jobs outside the factory walls and into their lives until they were no longer capable of accessing their artistic abilities. The factory essentially divorced them from their sense of their essential selves. This wouldn't happen to me, I thought, and moved to a large city to foster my skills as an artist and to surround myself with like-minded people. For many years this was feeling right, that I was doing exactly what I came to do, not working in the factory back home. But in 2005 when visiting my family for a reunion I listened again to their stories about the factory, and as always these stories saddened me. On the train ride home I had an epiphany that I had been treating my poetry like a factory, an assembly line, and doing so in many different ways, from how I constructed the poems, to my tabbed and sequenced folders for submissions to magazines, etc. This was a crisis, and I stopped writing for nearly a month, needing to figure out how to climb out of these factory-like structures, or to quit writing altogether. But I wanted to thrive in the crisis rather than end the trajectory of self-discovery the poems had set me on over the years. One morning I made a list of the worst problems with the factory, and at the top of that list was "lack of being present." The more I thought about this the more I realized this was what the factory robbed my family of the most, and the thing that frightened me the most, this not being aware of place in the present. That morning I started what I now call (Soma)tics, ritualized structures where being anything but present was next to impossible. These rituals create what I refer to as an "extreme present" where the many facets of what is around me wherever I am can come together through a sharper lens. It has been inspiriting that (Soma)tics reveal the creative viability of everything around me. This book contains twenty-three new (Soma)tic rituals and their resulting poems.

My deepest gratitude to everyone at Wave Books,
CAConrad

ECODEVIANCE

M.I.A. ESCALATOR

FOR JEN BENKA & CAROL MIRAKOVE

I rode several of my favorite escalators in Philadelphia, taking notes up and down the vantages. At the top and bottom of the ride I would show photographs of myself to strangers and ask, "EXCUSE ME, have you seen this person?" Sometimes there was confusion, "ISN'T THAT YOU?" I would reply, "No, many people think I look like HER, but have you seen HER?" I feel very fortunate to have been born BEFORE the ultrasound machine. My generation was the last generation to have a male and female name waiting at the other end of the birth canal. My generation is the last to have our mothers touch their bellies talking to us as male and female. Pink or blue?

Both pink and blue, "Have you seen this person?" I enjoyed my conversations with strangers and made at least one new friend, a handsome man who knew I was the person in the photograph. That person, I am that person and agreed. The ultrasound machine gives the parents the ability to talk to the unborn by their gender, taking the intersexed nine-month conversation away from the child. The opportunities limit us in our new world. Encourage parents to not know, encourage parents to allow anticipation on either end. Escalators are a nice ride, slowly rising and falling, writing while riding, notes for the poem, meeting new people at either end, "Excuse me, EXCUSE ME ..." My escalator notes became a poem.

I HOPE I'M LOUD

WHEN I'M DEAD

I have a
mannequin for
a paperweight
it is difficult to
type with such a
large paperweight
I reach around
lovers late into
night typing
from behind it is
impossible to
tell which
is Virgil
poetry
can be
of use
the field of flying
bullets the hand
reaches through
loving the aftertaste
finding a deeper
third taste
many are
haunted by
human cruelty through
the centuries
I am haunted by

our actions since
breakfast
you said *too much poetry*
I said *too much war*
the biggest mistake for
love is straining
there was a
door marked
MISTAKE we
entered
you said *too much fooling around*
I said *fuck off and die*

PRETERNATURAL CONVERSATIONS

FOR DANA WARD

Every once in a while I think something about a stranger on the sidewalk and they dart a glance at me and I get it—I GET IT—we are one! Allow seven consecutive days for this exercise. DAY ONE, think about a woman you know, think about experiences you have had with her. Think about conversations you have had, think about the things she wears, eats, her way of walking, her laugh. Think about every detail you can imagine. See if she calls you or e-mails you. Take notes about this attempt at psychic connection.

DAY TWO, do everything you did in DAY ONE, but for a man you know. DAY THREE, go out to the streets and follow someone walking a dog. Look closely at the dog, study the dog's movements. Whistle in your head, bark in your head. Imagine throwing a stick, yelling "GOOD DOG! GOOD DOG! YOU ARE A VERY GOOD DOG!" Does the dog respond to this? If so, how? Take notes.

DAYS FOUR, FIVE, SIX, and SEVEN are for strangers. In cafés or restaurants, or followed briefly on the sidewalk. Try to connect with two women and two men, complete strangers out in the world. Study them in cafés, museums, going up escalators, or maybe standing in line at the bank. Aim your attention at the clothing they wear or the way they chew food. Envision saying HELLO, tugging their sleeve. TUG IT with your mind, punctuated with putting an imaginary hand on their shoulder and saying, "Don't I know you?" Imagine clapping and shouting "HEY! HEY! HEY YOU!" Did they look at you WHILE you were walking behind them? Communicating beyond the auditory is our goal. What are their reactions? How do you feel about it? Take these seven days of notes and form your poem(s).

ONE

i'm going in for
a CAT scan i
mean an audition
for an opera
will it finally
break into
Two paths
this suffering One is tiresome
every gentle piece
of marble in
the sun was
once beaten
into shape
this doesn't
work with people
take many deep
breaths maybe
breathing can help
Jesus didn't
need balance
he had nails

TWO

i don't offer
frayed blooms while
caring for the center
i love my liver
my gallbladder
pat them good
morning through flesh
i want to show my
kidneys this sunrise
they deserve it working
hard take them out OUCH
see the pretty red
and pink OUCH sky
love you love you
sew you back
my spirit starts
chiming into the wind my
craving for wonder

THREE

i make a pie in
my own image
doorknob carried
in bag for months
open open opening
NOT a single thing
but
when public
toilet seat is
warm from
previous ass do you
become comforted
or leap off
in fear?
love is the
function of
time is the
discovery
this dream
pays for its
space in
my heart

FOUR

Ed Dorn says
faggots should drink directly
from the sewer
i want to dress
special for this
finger wilderness
in his beard
I.V. drip of
sphinx's blood
"what camouflage
will you wear to hide
in the gingerbread
house?" he asks
"none, I want the witch
to find me EAT ME!"
i prefer a song where
i am fed, "Oh Ed,
if you can't handle
me calling you my
sister I don't need
a brother"

FIVE

neckties
lynch my spirit
meet me against
morning silos which
do not happen
in Philadelphia
i need a soda to
wash this glitter down
it's dark in the stomach
next morning
bathroom light catches
glint of turd covered
in glitter
disco log in the bowl
fecal poetry ranges from
shocking to absurd
this is neither
this is pragmatic
it's my life as i need to live it
Ed Dorn i would hate myself if
i were you but i'm not and
get to live this spectacular
life of sparkling hygiene

SIX

in my
scary time
black letters
vanish in
the blue
the living
GIANTS
of Earth
are trees
keeping time by the thistle
to season weeds and their
sensual goals
a new kind of sparrow
shoots from my fears
chide it into a
cloud of itself
a golden needle
stitches my head to
my knee leaving me
aching along the river
STOP telling me damage can
ameliorate our lives
STOP trying to include
me in your portrait of
quietly dying poets

SEVEN

if i had been
there when they
invented the word
chair
things would
be different would sound better
look at this amazing
structure holding
our bodies in place
to write
to quarrel with ourselves and others
to eat and sing
to launch forth new ideas
to comfort the sphincter
chair is a ridiculous word
monosyllabic NONSENSE
i love chairs but remain
annoyed by their name
living in this post-vocabulary
chosen without
imagination
chair chair chair CHAIR
nothing less than
seven syllables will do

EQUINOX EVE

SILENT MEETING GROUP

FOR ALLISON COBB & JENNIFER COLEMAN

Over seven billion human beings live on Earth now. We have displaced or made extinct so many other species of animals, insects, and plants that we have actually lost track! In the age of Emily Dickinson less than a billion humans were alive and wild bison roamed the open plains of the United States. Today there is just a small herd grazing in Yellowstone National Park, and those were put there to be wild on purpose. Same with the wolves, also exterminated from the land, and now reintroduced by way of the park system. These animals are not wild they are museums of fur, hooves, and fangs, part of a well-managed safari rather than wilderness. We love our museums, they comfort and soothe us when we feel uncertain of the choices we have made.

This (Soma)tic ritual gets us a little closer to how strange and troubled we humans are. I made a flier and hung it all over Philadelphia:

SILENT MEETING GROUP
WEDNESDAY, MARCH 20TH
5PM TO 6PM
2ND FLOOR COUCH AREA OF
THE BOOK TRADER
(2ND ST. & MARKET ST.)
ONLY RULE: NO TALKING

There are only a few places where strangers can respectably be together in silence: on an elevator, at the movies, waiting for a bus, waiting to pay at the store. But to come together for the purpose of being quiet, to study one another for a full hour, that is something very different. As much as 80 percent of human communication is nonverbal, remember this detail. Do not fear looking at the people who show up because we all came to look and be looked at.

Twelve people participated, some of them quite odd looking, and one young Goth teen who glared at us with a sneer. Several were uncomfortable at the ten-minute mark, and they closed their eyes to meditate, or to appear to be meditating, but their eyes were closed for the rest of the hour. As soon as the hour was up I casually walked away WITH-OUT TALKING! It's important to GO, GET GOING, GO SOMEWHERE where you can sit and quietly take account of your silent meeting. Take the quiet with you to write your poem.

ECODEVIANCE

dear glen of
goldenrod
I would have
your abortion
not being devoted to the way
things appear
you want me to
be fearless but
I cannot relax in
your world I can
go home where
success collides with
all the bad
behavior that
fed me to the
tyranny of the
chrysalis
you ask if
Shakespeare
was queer
I say the love of
his Juliet and his
Romeo was as
outlaw as it gets
devoted to the way
things are means the
odds are bad
sometimes white men
with long hair nod to

me downtown because
I'm a white man with
long hair
    you think
    having your
    abortion means
    I love you
    what can
    I say

UNKNOWN DURATION OF FEAR

FOR DAWN LUNDY MARTIN

How we spend our days is, of course, how we spend our lives. —ANNIE DILLARD

No matter how many human beings are born to overflow the land, we are still careful to touch. We are careful with the touching. On an eight-hour flight I took notes about a man pressed against my arm. There are so many men and I know almost none of them, even this one whose forearm heat mixed with my forearm heat. He slept, quietly snoring, dreaming, then jumping awake in his seat, looking to recognize me from the dream? From the airport? His face said, *"Who is this?"*

People he loved knew him in the past, the past being as much as an hour ago, and would know him again in the future. But in the present he slouched against me and no one he loved was there to see him breathing the smaller breaths of a body taking down to rest. No matter how many human beings are born to push plants and animals off the planet, we only permit touching strangers in a few locations: crowded subways, buses, airplanes. You do not touch a stranger at the checkout counter, unless it's an accident, and then you apologize, sorry, say sorry. You cannot touch a stranger at the restaurant. You are not going to hold the stranger's hand while they cut meat because you will be called insane and asked to leave. If you refuse to leave, if you refuse to stop holding their hand, the police will be called. But if you know them, a little, you can shake their hand Hello and all is well. If you are close friends you get a hug. If you are lovers you can taste and smell each other and this is a marvelous thing the world awaits.

When he woke a little startled I waved my turquoise-glitter fingernails. Glitter twinkling in lamplight, his eyes caught by glitter, smiling and nodding. What a nice smile a stranger can have. My notebook was small to conceal my notes for the poem, notes on the experience of pressing against a man for eight hours, never to see him again. Will he remember the glitter? How could he possibly forget? There is no way to prevent the cost of living a day as the loss of that day, closer all the time to no more days. Death pisses me off, and I want strangers to know this about me. I will make a sign HONK IF DEATH PISSES YOU OFF and they will honk even though we don't know one another. There's just not enough time to know us all. My goal is to relax with you, stranger, to not fear grabbing your hand at the doorway and introducing myself with a poem.

A HUMAN BEING REALIZES
THEY ARE ALONE FOR THE
FIRST TIME IN 12 HOURS

to appropriate our
dreaming together
we no longer asked
for our deliverance
generation gap of archetypes
climb the clown
known as the
clown ladder
a new channel to count on
a better system for exploding
when you open the case do not
look for my love
I am sorry
you are too
the what of the
conversation eludes all day
generation gap of drag queens malcontented
generation gap of bean sprout and bean
together in my mouth
leaning on a freshly
dressed lamb
rubbing season
into neck and shoulders
I would love you if I knew how to make the song
a better system lit from the edges

take a second to calm down
maybe another
Okay
okay
giant living surface for these placements
once there was a ball full of dust and we
let it roll off
goodbye

SUSPENSION FLUID
MAGNIFICENCE

FOR SAMUEL R. DELANY & STEPHEN BOYER

When I was given my first rifle at nine my friend Chris and I went into the woods. I was a good shot and skinned and cleaned the squirrel in the creek and cooked him over a small fire. This was the first meal I fully provided myself, my *Lord of the Flies* afternoon, something to measure against the world.

How is wilderness memorized into the body? What lens does it provide? I went to where the wild is mostly hidden. At lunch hour I walked around JFK Blvd. in Philadelphia where men in suits poured out of skyscrapers in search of meat.

It was at busy street corners where I found most of my study participants. I would ask, "Excuse me sir, on a scale from 1 to 5, 1 being thin and creamy, and 5 being cottage cheese, how do you rate your semen?"

One man grabbed me and THREW ME against a light pole, "GET OUT OF HERE YOU FUCKING FAGGOT!!" How thrilling!! I was told to fuck off, called a faggot a handful of times, told I was SICK, a degenerate. While all of this is interesting, I was looking for the few men who would step up to the quiet, feral interior.

Finally one man said, "I'm a 3."
ME: 3, okay. (writing in my notebook) So that's thick and creamy?
MAN: Yes, no curd, HAHA!!
ME: Very interesting.
MAN: Thanks for asking.
ME: Thanks for answering.

Another man wanted to know whether anyone answered 5. We wondered whether some-one rating their semen a 5 is unwell, or not eating properly. Semen is fascinating as far as suspension fluids on Earth go, created and produced with extreme pleasure. The orgasm the flash of light reconnecting to the original proliferation of cells and the construction of sensate flesh, which is a very marvelous thing, being here, all of us. My notes from the boulevard of quiet, feral interiors became a poem.

IF NO ONE COMES TO SAVE YOU

IT'S BECAUSE OF TELEVISION

carried away by fleas
one drop at a time
quick nod to the
doorman like we
belong here
tooth-bearing sides to
a job no one can frame
juries of the middle-sized storm
itching and finking for another golden seesaw
formula for taking the season and turning it into a pie

pleasure in hard times gives us relief
until we all belong to the song
we were crying in the meadow
but that was never the worry
this thing catches up with us
we dream inside each other
literally and I've wanted to
be lost in this friend you are
grunting to the will
of coming beasts

things mark themselves off for order
until something expires in the order
we're going to end this now there's
nothing more nerves can haggle over

SECURITY CAMERAS AND FLOWERS DREAMING THE ELEVATION ALLEGIANCE

FOR SUSIE TIMMONS

From Walnut & Broad St. to Walnut & 19th I stopped for every security camera. Philadelphia watches us always, FUCK YOU WATCHING US ALWAYS!! Several cameras in one block. I took notes, it was noon it was twelve just as I wanted it to be. I took notes for the poem, notes notes notes.

A little basket of edible flowers: nasturtiums, roses, pansies. I eat pansies, I LOVE pansies, they're delicious buttery purple lettuce!! At each security camera I paused, looked into the camera, DIRECTLY IN THERE, and stuck my tongue inside a flower. Flicked it in and out, in and out, flicking, licking, suckling blossoms. A security guard asked, *"What the fuck are YOU DOING?"* I replied, "I'M A POLLINATOR, I'M A POLLINATOR!!" I allowed myself to say only this for the duration of the security camera pollination application, "I'M A POLLINATOR, I'M A POLLINATOR!!" I took many notes, and the notes became a poem titled, "I WANT TO DO EVERY / THING WRONG JUST ONCE."

I WANT TO DO EVERY
THING WRONG JUST ONCE

suddenly we are
a daisy under
the big wheel
throw it out to the batter leave it up to the outfield
the umpire sees how I divide you from me
you have no choice over the
weak notes in the song
you think I'm afraid
of course I am
I'm disgusted chopping us in two
will it help to
kill the one who
hypnotizes you?
we can try
we can always try
betting on the better point of quaking
we cap the balding yard with angel wings ancient astronauts
a poetic acuity we have been waiting to carry us away forever
to survive I stayed away from
people who wanted to
kill me (that's
the big secret)
let them jam it
in the back of your
mouth just a quick
police search

SCRYER'S INVITATION

FOR HOA NGUYEN

Having lived with a ghost for more than a decade I knew where he hovered and settled into walls and lights. This is where I aimed my scrying mirror. I sat on the floor with a handheld mirror and a larger one behind me. The point was to be able to see the larger mirror behind me with the smaller handheld one. The ghost is named Owen. He lived next door and killed himself where my new neighbor brushes his teeth each morning. Owen was 21; he liked books and used to work at Rizzoli's bookshop on Broad St. here in beautiful Philadelphia. He has heard me read many poems by others since his death. I would say, "OH, Owen, this is beautiful, listen to THIS!"

Late at night, blocking all light from windows I read Hoa Nguyen's book *AS LONG AS TREES LAST*. By candlelight I read a poem out loud, saying, "OWEN, THE POEM IS TITLED 'RAGE SONNET' AND SOUNDS LIKE THIS . . ." At the end of each poem I snuffed the candle to peer into the mirror behind me through the handheld mirror. I stared for a long time, dark to dark. Then the next poem by Hoa, "OWEN, THE POEM IS TITLED 'I'M STUCK' AND SOUNDS LIKE THIS . . ."

Finally there was a face in the mirror. After a long, assiduous stare I saw my face with another behind, then above. Was I imagining this? I can't say. The last book Owen read when he was alive was *MOBY-DICK*. When I told his mother she said, "That's a children's book isn't it?" I said, "No ma'am, it's not, not at all." Tonight I'm here, with poetry by Hoa Nguyen, being productive with a ten-year suicide, but making sense is the last thing on my mind. By candlelight my note taking and poem reading, "I have thought for / a dirty starved circle" until the ghost and I were finished, and Hoa was finished. My (Soma)tic notes forming into a poem, thank you Hoa, thank you Owen!!

LET IF DRIVE THE CONVERSATION

wings we paint on
kite are how we
wonder for the sky
a bone of shade
we get excited and
then it's just another
melted popsicle
remainder of the
sex act is nothing
you lean in on me for
the coasting
reputed to be the best
path to take in death
just take it and shut up sleeping in your corpse
it's okay to let it happen like this
you don't know how to
need it back and that's fine
cardamom-tanged lover
break off little bits for us
something we can come at again
right in the face *Glock it up man*
all the great leaders pulled
tonsils extracting some lasting words
pin us up on the board with
the rest of your receipts
I want to hang there
bathe in the grunts of
your woeful fraternity
open the senses and

let us begin to begin
let it all belong in here
sometimes a cock up
your ass is all it
takes to get the
point across
the made in china
sticker pulled away to
reveal the made
up in your
head sticker

QUARTZ CRYSTAL SHAKESPEARE SONNET TRANSLATION

FOR PAUL LEGAULT & SHARMILA COHEN

Piezoelectricity has proved the capacity quartz crystal has as a battery for electrical charge as well as its ability to store and transmit information. Let's take it a step further, a step FORWARD! Purchase a small clear quartz crystal. Set it in a bowl of salt overnight to clean it. When you wake, flush the salt down the toilet, rinse your quartz, and DON'T LET ANYONE put their hands on it from now on. It's YOUR crystal, don't even let them SEE IT!

Choose one of Mr. Shakespeare's sonnets for an English-to-English translation, or have someone choose one for you. Paul Legault and Sharmila Cohen chose sonnet #6 for me. I translated two lines a day for seven days by holding my crystal to my mouth like a walkie-talkie to whisper the lines, SHOUT THE LINES. Several times every hour I STOPPED, held my crystal to my mouth and spoke into it, "Then let not winter's ragged hand deface / In thee thy summer, ere thou be distill'd:" JUST LIKE THAT! Tell your crystal the lines over and over throughout the day. "THEN LET NOT WINTER'S RAGGED HAND DEFACE / IN THEE THY SUMMER, ERE THOU BE DIS-TILL'D:" Years ago in a dream I found an enormous cluster of crystals emerging from a forest floor. A voice whispered to me, "Crystals are the bones of the Earth." I talk to our planet's crystal bones! So can you!

At night I instructed the crystal to PLEASE translate the lines for me in a dream. Programming our crystals is our right as citizens of the Milky Way, but they respond best with PLEASE and THANK YOU! In the morning, before rising, I placed my crystal on my forehead and meditated for a few minutes, lying quite still. Then I picked up pen and paper and wrote the first two lines that came to mind. Then I thanked the crystal, and started over with the next two lines.

TELL US WHEN SOMETHING
IS HAPPENING OR WE
MIGHT NOT KNOW

calories of mink dust and champagne
my gay minstrel show grows dark and bloody
too bad I left the lion-taming chair at home
my hope you fly through the door
my hope you fly through the window
we need you WHERE HAVE YOU GONE?
but for the sex good enough for poetry
love not me but the rind falling from my mouth
cradle of injury winging past the hearth
emancipate one tired shard by dawn
lumber is a tree
pork chop is a pig
is mean
is mean

ARBOREAL CRYSTAL ARIA

FOR MARIANNE MORRIS

Find a plant, tree, some living nonhuman entity you want to communicate with. For me it was a giant sycamore tree in Philadelphia, a tree I've known for years. I cleaned my quartz crystal by resting it on a shallow bed of sea salt overnight. I touched the tree with my left hand while speaking into my crystal in my right hand, "PLEASE translate any messages my tree friend has for me." I then touched the tree with my right hand while holding on to the crystal with my left hand. I stayed this way for fifteen minutes, quiet, with eyes closed, letting the communication course through me and into the crystal for processing. My hands grew HOT.

As soon as I opened my eyes I began taking notes. I asked the crystal, "Was there a question for me, please say." I heard "NOTHING!" The word rang through me. Trees don't need to ask us anything, but they have plenty to tell us and I let my crystal tell me and let the notes flow out of me. What will it take to recognize the intelligence of such a quiet giant? Years ago I was leaning against the tree, earnestly writing a Frank poem, and suddenly looked up into the branches who seemed to shake with no wind, and I HEARD the anger aimed at my pen carving into paper, paper made of tree, wood. There I was, the human carving my own thoughts in my oblivious imperialism. What love do I really have outside my own kind of animal? I took many notes for a poem through the crystal translations of a tree.

EVERYTHING'S CALLED SOMETHING
ELSE BEFORE IT'S CALLED FAMINE

we're experiencing an
awkward font moment in
the text today a place in
history my
country will
not escape
vase of polyester blooms and
poets weakening poetry with despair
hold on we are a sign a doll
through a rip in the
carpet of clouds
buildings fill on
sad workers
the giant
knocked on the
ninth-floor window
we opened curtains
without thinking how
we needed one another
our latent sentences
breaking into songs
the first time you
shit your pants as an
adult remember to
understand the
baby crying

we are centuries from
bearing the proper love
we let carts go downhill on
their own smash smash smash
there is nothing now
nothing nothing nothing
we won't do to be
a soundtrack for the
sunlight brigade

FULL MOON HAWK APPLICATION

FOR FRANK SHERLOCK

everlastingly stronger
on top of the moon
—ALFRED STARR HAMILTON

I had the privilege of spending a month in the Leighton Artist Colony's Hemingway Studio at Banff Centre, located in the Canadian Rockies. In ancient times First Nations people used Banff as a locus for healing their sick, but they refused to live there. Banff Centre sits atop an enormous deposit of magnetic iron. Many holistic health practitioners use magnets to pull toxins out of the tissue and into the blood to then be flushed from the body. Here we are catching up with ancestral wisdom, finally.

This (Soma)tic poetry ritual resulted in a series of apologue poems without a definitive statement, the moral caught in a fang in a tree. Every morning I would meditate on a Philadelphia webcam poised on redtail hawks and their three chicks nesting on a window ledge of the Benjamin Franklin Institute. It was ridiculous leaving Philadelphia to visit it via webcam every single morning in western Canada, but the ridiculous world's exertions is what I sought to unzip the sublime. I wrote inside the hawk application, writing through the Philadelphia webcam. One day my boyfriend Rich appeared on the camera, waving from the street below the nest, then opened his sign FUCK YOU COME HOME!

A young man named Freddie drove me to the top of the mountains above the art colony to show me the hot springs and lake. There were fish in the lake, fish swimming above our heads at Banff Centre, and this became part of my (Soma)tic ritual. I would go to sleep with a piece of celestite crystal, meditating on the swimming above me, *the swimming above me! OREAD FREQUENCIES!* The notes for the poems were often informed by nightmares, the magnetic iron dumping toxins into my blood, making sleep difficult. A few nights it seemed I didn't sleep at all, but was instead dreaming about not sleeping. Once I dreamed I had a cunt for a nose, and that was fantastic, putting fingers in the cunt of my face!

After notes from the morning hawk webcam meditations I brushed my gums vigorously with cayenne pepper to stimulate the capillaries, JOLT the heart. I then drank a glass of crystal-infused water, the glass flanked by a four-inch shaft of citrine, a two-inch pyramid of selenite, and dangling just above the surface was a piece of the ancient Russian meteorite known as seraphinite. The citrine and selenite pulled negative charge from the water while seraphinite infused it with the angelic order to trigger my spinal cord into epiphanic alignment.

Mountain lion paw prints in fresh snow, grizzly bear scat, elk, mink, a pack of beautiful coyotes, and the magnificent magpies were outside my studio in the forest. It would be easy to write nature poems, documentary poems, straight-up narrative poems, but my notes were for poems found in the greasy film along the engines of our planetary machine coughing, devouring, running in terror. My unease of hungry mountain lions, grizzlies, and angry elk fueled the notes. A strict vegan diet with deep-tissue shiatsu massage once a week also contributed to the lens I brought to the notes for the poems. Banff was scraping me clean each day, and I kept to the flow, kept the image of fish swimming above my head, the hawks feeding their young, and the crystals I slept with on the full moon for the final hawk application. The notes became 13 poems for 13 moons. The editing process for the poems included listening to three original movie soundtracks played simultaneously: *Paris Texas*, *The Assassination of Jesse James*, and *Brokeback Mountain*.

READING STARLIGHT
WITH ONE EYE
LIKE CREELEY

hearing all bells at
once instructs the final exhale
Camelot in thimble of the gods
Marilyn Monroe's ambulance
lost on the way to the palace of temperament
a branch of government for the magical arts
punch wall of forest for
an oaken
desk
another dream we
needed agitating the
sentence as it rows across a
newly destroyed heart folding
following tormenting one another
we were all once young and
beautiful squandering everything
it's what we came here to do
cut off engines to the child
registering disposition of
cat in the dark as the
size of the darkness

DID YOU EVER FORGET
SOMEONE CAN'T HELP YOU
BECAUSE THEY'RE DEAD
I'M BORING LIKE THAT

we can never oversimplify the
way it will occur making me
friend like a friend in the dark
my plot to cover the place with tenderness
a planet coping with seven billion
human breaths a second no
exit route planned not sure
if what we do to live will
smash us to dust
hawks washing through our veins
tongues pressed to spiderwebs
I love the way we are
high together trying to
shout ourselves off the
map *this is dangerous* you say
I hit the fallen snow with a
banana over and over chanting
THIS TROPICAL FRUIT NOW KNOWS THE ICE CRYSTAL
THIS TROPICAL FRUIT NOW KNOWS THE ICE CRYSTAL
THIS TROPICAL FRUIT NOW KNOWS THE ICE CRYSTAL
THIS TROPICAL FRUIT NOW KNOWS THE ICE CRYSTAL

ALL THE BOOKS

HOLDING BACK

OUR ENEMIES

my integument
breach is substantial
not to brag
killing off the coastline
I can't stop myself from
butchering it all
your smell is nice
keep me under your coat awhile
you are warmer than I have ever been
smell better than I have ever smelled
ask anybody outside this
intermediate station of
the waist-high demon
garlands of dead
children for the pentagon
catharsis is a daughter
a son a caterwaul
soon we fall apart we
were hoping to do so
vomit in folders with
the purple tabs
vocabulary after
death has a different
present tense
vowels out of range

ENOUGH COCAINE

FOR A SNOW ANGEL

burning inside the
box is a thinking to
make holes in
a noun
I worry about gravy my body will
produce in the crematorium
is this embarrassment morbid
am I supposed to
apologize I never
know when it's
time for sorry
I'm tired of fucking around we need
action is that the right thing to need
ebullience of being a lion tonight
I'm coming at you my dear
get the whip get the chair
look scared look scared
no meat no meat
throw me broccoli
throw me kale
green pussy
green green green pussy
I'm gonna be
green pussy

WHO PUNISHES US
MORE THAN THE SAD
EYES OF OUR VICTIMS

when humans
trust weeds
know them
hear
tone of grass see visions of
milking their blades to
blend with ordinary
gentleness of wind
ketamine has
nothing on my
dreaming it's a good
time some other
bastard can have
this planet
is what they
told us it would be
a French pair of French fervency
scent of delicious French armpits
Alice paused to face Gertrude
you know how to grab me throw me under
your indelicate disposition you are like
swallowing a needle in search of thread
but you won't put that in your
book of what you say I say

CATHODE OF OUR

CONNECTION

instead of a million
dollars this poem is
gratis carrying a pinch
of hair after the
funeral eight of my
eggs deposited in
your coffin you
would approve you
would approve your
voice cracked thermometer
at once a fitted gift thickening as
it calms in the bright demonic firma
a patient tap of light on the shoulder
leaving the gun at home for a change
we came up here like this and now
nothing suits us poems inking our
way back through thickets hoping
the soft breeze coming this
way will let us be loved
no no no
don't see
me just yet
flickering by
cigarette light

WE ARE GOLD
COINS TURNING
IN SUNLIGHT

a limb of fortune called the
last thing you will know
is rubber it stretches
when I was 47 this morning
my crayons hit a map of
the united states forecasting an
end to self pity and war crimes
how can you stand me
how can you keep
sleeping with me
well I wouldn't
things are not
what you expected
nor will they ever be again
what it forsakes we bring to
another shoulder
old bones
as in now
not later
coming like this to
the end of the planet
the adhesive my body produces from
too much worry generous amounts to
seal the files for good

COPING SKILLS LOST
IN THE FLOOD

we're
aching upwards of a
teenage broken phone
hearing underwater
libraries up the side of
the dinner plate
a little too fast
not ungrateful like
some of these bastards around here
can't tap out a tune with you looking away
genies of not enough sleep
a happier location for
the war not the
easiest thing you realize
beautiful architecture
refreshing beverages
our sign reads *hello love us for*
the century of
progress we
gave you
bombers
arriving
early here
they are

BUILT TO SHAKE
OURSELVES AWAKE

squid as verb
the recurring dream
squid as examination tool
squid as prefix to love and
other used kisses tasting new
WHAT IS THIS panting I do at
the foot of the giant
waiting for a little
junkyard freedom
a stone my meanest calling card
a seed hammered into my trigger to draw
you near the middle of what I need going
over thighs with gusto
feeling brush of a
passing god is all it
takes to start the new
way of keeping our lives
squid squeal and
cry as suffix to
fixing the
smallest
needs
a fruitful
gateway to proper
rejuvenating rest

CHILDREN KNOW MOUTH OF
FABLE PILOTS THE WAY
TO WOMB SNOUT

he woke with a
vagina instead of a
nose some women walked by pointing
how does that smell they asked
everything smells redundant or
like everything at once
it's not a super nose it's
a cunt nose they said
makes me see things
then slow in the throat
now we are arriving
wake in middle of this
poem forged in the encampment
comes with a split sensation
all I ever wanted
was to be tiny
fit in your
pocket
does this
creep you out
sounds like
your problem

PERMISSION PLEASE

TO BE A STONE

BUT YOU ARE A

CLOCK WE SAY

over a billion
tears an hour the human
race will drown you on
the wrong street
romance slipping
incinerator above a
marriage means no
counseling is feasible
no wonder clocks aspire to granite
following landscapes of fervor
sword by bed seemed to
make sense last night
part of the wall changed part of
the story in blood splatters
promising growth spurt in
the forest of
your thighs
don't allude to my spurt
don't look at my thighs
you pernicious clocks
make the worst stones

TO AGREE WITH
NOTHING YOUR
NEIGHBORS SAY
IS LONELY

a new
constitution for
all dogs in the yard
a body drills into the
resources by picking up a package
use me it says *go ahead use me*
advantages of keen sensory
the outcome you want with
more toothpaste commercials
leaning into nubile encounters
a choice coin spills from the cup
please please please before
we're obliged to concede to
alternate paths climbing
raiment of the goddess
our master of slaying
come back to the cellar
caroling pitched into
millennial refrain
keeps us freer than
the rest of them is all we care in
our mercenary nation of villains

LONELY DEEP

AFFECTION

years of practice for a soft
landing in the slaughter
we looked far off to
a flag sewn into flesh
dear enemy come down the
hill I have taken a title out
of the love for you jumping
down the clear shaft of your eye
you would not know how long I
paused when writing this unless
I said so in the poem
half an hour staring
at the pencil having
written of my enemy with
love and fight to maintain
the ascension
voices from a
room no one exits
we pry genocide out
of the museum but
meant to remove
the museum
from genocide

PAINTED PIGEON PROJECT

FOR CANDICE LIN

Find a photograph of a bird living far from where you live. I received a photo of a beautiful, truly extraordinary pigeon who lives near the Rialto Bridge in Venice. She has turquoise, chartreuse, and other shades of green and blue, painted with food coloring by artists. Print the photo and flutter it above your head, hold it to trees, rocks, ledges, imagining, imagining, imagining!! I painted my hand colors of the Venetian beauty, cooing when hand snuggled inside a pocket. I took notes while eating seeds offered from my pigeon hand. Pigeon hand is not a condition any more than art is a condition.

Save hair from your brush and roll it into a nice soft ball, then wash it. Insert a few seeds of flax, pumpkin, and caraway, something delicious. Pour more seeds on the ground, hair tucked in the center. Wait and watch. Soon enough a bird will carry it off to cushion their nest. Try to be patient and watch for them, try to see them. Write down EXACTLY what they looked like, where they flew off to, and keep that writing on you at all times. Take it out of your pocket and read it. Read it before going off to sleep at night. DREAM of the nest by thinking about these small, feathered creatures sleeping on your hair, and touch your hair while falling off to sleep, you and the birds, sleeping and dreaming together. WAKE and write as fast as you can, WAKE and write, wake and WRITE!! The notes become the poem.

NOW ONLY 30% TAPHEPHOBIC

FEELING BETTER BY OPEN HOLES

future war
pains me to
touch off this
diving board
drawn to make it living
you said we must not think of a gloomy world
we must not live in the present I think you mean
will angle with bees in the field
will explore child's mind in math lab
someone shatters their heart at
the microphone and we
go with them a bunch of
maudlin spectators we can't
leave it inside the sentence
pull it off the paper make a
door in woodshop shut it out
babies born in war melt out of this hell
stop them from entering the sentence
the only man I wanted to
grow old with was killed in
the hills of Tennessee
dreaming head to head
across night together
whistles branding
air around us
ordered in the execrable
another near miss of mortar shell

I blame everyone when I blame
myself I'm that good a shot
fuck you we got you now
gangster coffin with a
presidential seal may you keep
fleeing the underworld in vain
farmers of the patch of clean white
paper what made you spell my
     name before I was ready
     too bad too bad too bad
     mom did jesus have pubes
     jesus didn't have a cock honey

CORMORANT STAGECRAFT

FOR CAITLIN LACOURSE RYAN & KEPLER-22B

Venturing into the sun to smoke
I am proof of nature and all its declarations.
—ARIANA REINES

Kitten is my principal spirit animal, a totem to conquer my various forgivable, discordant planes of constriction. But it is the cormorant I surrender to for my most morbid of human needs. A cormorant DIVES into subconscious water-worlds to resurface somewhere new, and agitates my soul into happiness. When I was a boy I yearned for webbed fingers and toes, and was grateful to Benjamin Franklin for inventing swim flippers. When I was telling Ryan Eckes about this new (Soma)tic ritual he said, "That's what I try to do with every poem, I try not to drown."

What animal will you require yourself to meet for this exercise? I wore nylon stockings on my hands, then DOVE into the morning ocean off Virginia Beach, American fighter jets howling across the coastal trails, deafening the gulls, frightening the dolphins, and me. Eggs in the sand, nest in the dunes, a wind where all instruction flattens my eager crest. Love in a cormorant call compels a vibratory trance throughout a feral heart, lungs, liver.

Draw eight pictures of your spirit animal in different phases of your enactment of their lives. On the back of each write a message. Write a bit of confession from the bird, hippo, or unicorn you choose to be. Create an e-mail account for this exercise to include at the end of the message. Leave the pictures on the subway, in the bathroom at a museum, or the coffee shop counter. Anyone who writes you must receive your animal's reply. Your animal correspondence is YOUR TRUE correspondence! All your notes from the exercise become the poem.

WHAT IS BRIBERY IN
POETRY GOING TO PROVE

I claim a hundred feet of
air above my head
making use of tiny instruments needing
their music absorbed
roller coasters are
my favorite form
of transportation
elevating harmed
avionics of the brain
climbING tracks
ROARing downhill
reborn through the S-curve
love came breathing against me
I did not mind the captivity
pluck me out of my gown
throw me against your song
a murmur of sparrows
flew in flew out
keeping me
nauseated
with love
OH if I could take the
roller coaster across
town every day instead of the bus
I love being a statistic involving
spun sugar on a stick and instability
a thousand stories in a

thousand drops of saliva
we can read ANYTHING
go out and read the
engine's cold
throttle left overnight in one position
my endless attempts to
care about happiness
the extortion of poetry
an opera mounting the bedsheets
we won't stop it when we know we must
my critical review of your little daisy
staring staring staring staring
STARING until it grows

9 ADZUKI THOUGHTS

FOR LISA JARNOT

9 is an epiphany, the energy entering the bottom tip of the number, traveling up the stem and circulating in the crown.

I carried 9 adzuki beans with me for a day, talking to them one at a time, then as a group, then holding them to my ear with eyes closed. Hearing 9 uncertainties, 9 calls to ration sadness. They slept through the night with rose quartz in a jar of warm water. When I planted them I held them one at a time under the dirt, my eyes closed, tuning to a steady humming underground where bean pulses waken. Notes, notes, I took many notes all the while for the poem. When they sprouted I held them in my mouth one at a time. I sealed my ears with plugs, blocking any sound except my teeth chewing adzuki thoughts into my own. 9 thoughts for 9 requests for equilibrium, then more notes for the poem were taken.

ELLIPSIS ON ELLIPSIS UNTIL THE
ROOM IS DARKENED WITH INK

taste birth canal
where the mob is going to hang him
the many excuses they will live with
to become nursery rhyme disturbing
some on-and-off switch in the face of
disaster back to the surface
remember to breathe
walked up these
steps to say
even though
you deserved
it I'm sorry
cover us in ketchup to
look like the
car wreck
we feel inside
the planet warmed
early warnings a
stammer came in
sounds of glaze and
cream needing brown
to cover the green
don't worry hear
colors tell us what is next
okay we made brown blackest blue
we lingered over the palate
long enough for
the single most
recognizable salt of
misery

TRANSLUCENT SALAMANDER

FOR EILEEN MYLES & RYAN ECKES

the cynic and the killer waltz together
—FROM A SONG MY GRANDMOTHER SANG

But I know someone must die. Something must be gained and something must
be lost. The stakes are now too high for us all to make up and go home.
There is a gun, there is a sword, and none of us can stop thinking about them.
—CHANA PORTER, from *Leap and the Net Will Appear*

Wyoming is the least inhabited of the fifty states. I was excited to see the night sky at Ucross Foundation. Each night I sat waiting for the stars. I noted the first and brightest above distant hills, above branches, and as others twinkled into view I created my own constellations. Eighteen in all, and each constellation demanded a different toll to pay at the start of my note taking. For instance the fifth toll of Xallan was paid by meditating with a fist of citrine stone in my left hand. The toll of stars over Ucross was always paid in meditating with stones. Labradorite, a gift from poet Bhanu Kapil, is a stone of the dark crone, enhancing inner passageways to bring light to the cancerous shadow-lands of a life. Celestite, purchased in Boulder, Colorado, is a gem used to communicate with spirit guides some call angels. Clear quartz, a gift from poet Elizabeth Willis, was a translucent mirror where the salamander appeared in a waking dream. The citrine I purchased at the Edgar Cayce Institute cleaned negative charge and led the way to understanding the wealth of this organic body named Ucross where deer, mink, golden eagles, sheep, rabbits, mice, and thousands of insects, plants, stones, worms, birds, and other living beings thrive in their own unimpeded cycles. One night a great horned owl dropped a mouse at my feet. I wrote, "it doesn't have to mean something / but it probably does." I would write my notes while staring into a constellation with a gemstone in my left hand. Not since my childhood in rural Pennsylvania have I spent this much time staring into the Milky Way. And as I did as a boy, I would STARE AT ONE STAR for as long as it took to SUD-DENLY SEE, for just a second, ALL OF THEM AT ONCE!!

Hammering the notes into one document the next morning started with drinking a drop of Lemurian quartz. Barry David of Mount Shasta makes gemstone infusions under the full moon with mountain spring water and crystal essence. This is the same crystal I wear around my neck, a Lemurian quartz. I also wore a rotating scent of sandalwood, cedar, and rose. Sandalwood has a high frequency that aligns the chakras and enhances cellular vibration for spiritual awareness. Cedar helps eliminate mental and spiritual obstructions and stagnation for clearer and more harmonious creative channels. Rose has the highest hertz measurements of any living being on Earth, and its scent will immediately clear the heart chakra, making it a portal for psychic transmission and reception. Each day I rotated these oils, a dab on the third eye, the wrists, the soles of my feet, and with a sip of Lemurian quartz I would BEGIN!!

At noon when lunch arrived I would take the fruit from the bag, set it on the floor with my laptop, then play one of the eight songs on the album *Cathedral City* by the musical genius of VICTOIRE, composed by Missy Mazzoli. The music of *Cathedral City* was perfect as a vehicle to channel my constellation notes into poems. I would cover the piece of fruit and laptop with a basket, then with a blanket, then with pillows, then with towels, and finally with a large comforter, then PLAY THE MUSIC AS LOUD AS I COULD. It was inaudible from all the coverings that were keeping the music CLOSE to the piece of fruit and INFUSING its water molecules with VICTOIRE!! As soon as the song was finished I ATE THE FRUIT as quickly as possible while the song was still deep inside its flesh. Eating song in fruit, EATING SONG!! I then set about with the first phase of dividing my notes into language for poetry. In the sunlight I would lie on my back, my head over the edge of the deck, to SEE the beautiful pastures and quaking aspen upside down. The upside-down view was for the second phase of dividing my notes into language for poetry. I would look back and forth between the upside-down beautiful world, and the notes, until the notes were picked clean of excrescence and the shining teeth came clear in the skull.

In late afternoon I would wash my crystals in peppermint soap and set them in the sun to dry and collect nutrient-rich light. A sheep I named Gabriella, after one of my constellations, would always approach her fence closest to the gemstones. One day a flock of agitated migrating starlings surrounded them, singing WILDLY into them!! For weeks the eighteen poems were created and later sculpted, one for each of my eighteen constellations over Wyoming skies. Part of my meditation wandered from the beauty of this natural setting to remember how it is people have destroyed so much land that Ucross seems an oasis. We have been mistaken for centuries about our lives on Earth. Early white men named Yosemite National Park, thinking it was the name of the native Miwok people who first lived there. Yosemite actually means "Killers, those to be feared." One of our great national parks is named after a description of who we have turned out to be, clawing our way through untold reserves of natural resources, killing all life that gets in the way.

HEAD OUT WINDOW ON

THE BAPTISM HIGHWAY

shake tall
buildings
out of my
loving you
down far down
far far down by a
rock at the water
finish cooking soup with
violins everything could use
a melody to set it right
mitigate suffering you
care you
cannot with
success deny
needing violins
okay trombones the
trombones enter the
pasta entering our bodies
the microscope shows
there is song between the grains
the wind the wheat endured is
a taste the
animal
carries forward
immersion of
hours through a
loosening bone

we are without the
timing of the beetle
a sound that cannot
get to where we left
our homes in shame

THE CHURCH OF MOSS
IN TERRA INCOGNITA

sharp angles of
the god tore my
pretty dress
kiss his barbed-wire mouth to
leave me alone *leave me alone*
rise in dark
rig the map to be
unrecoverable
ready to grow
into my hooves
no more butterfly disposed to
the metal pin
jactitation means both
false marriage and
twitching with illness
these days you envelop ENVELOP
until slashing your tires is
my only articulation
my blade always ready
to speak
bending time to
an agrarian impulse
genie of the globe makes a
pancake of her cities
loading answers into a
Smith & Wesson with
no questions asked

OPEN THE GATE!
we are hungry for
the little feast that
was promised
we won't
hear "no"

THE NERVE FOR HONEY
MUST PREVAIL

my antlers my antennae
touching
your
wall catching my name in a rumor
nice rumor
about falling
for the guy
a tinsel of
mending found in
the fossil record
every satisfied
customer agrees
the philter is a
liquid within
we have
case studies
doused in it
an aesthetic
armored
with it
anyone with
sense wants
madness to end wants
Canada to invade the
United States of
the Americas

bring us to our knees
dissolve our military
imprison our leaders
distribute our wealth
insist we live in peace

THE DREAM PART OF THIS WAS NEVER

HARRY'S OCCULT & SPIRITUAL SUPPLIES

ceilings are no good for chairs
but my drunk mother insists
throw me up some cigarettes
hurry what are you waiting for
I'm waiting for another messiah
one without nails
one who lacks the pressure of nails on Sunday
a messiah who can savor a
beautiful afternoon of
fucking without guilt
stupid Judas your sack of
gold under your swaying feet
something lives in these weeds
something twinkling something smart
much smarter than you and I
it's here this intelligence and it calms me
there are many reasons to be
afraid but I cannot think of one at the moment
if you are pro-life why are you
sending your son to war
bring the kid home
you stupid fuckup
he's left to your shadows
he's lost to your cursed compliance
tell them we are going to pull this
shit apart if they don't help us lift
it through the temple window

little gifts of days
as many as I can get
I'll ask only for
days from now on
every Christmas
especially Easter

BE A MONSTER TO ANYONE WHO IS CRUEL TO ANIMALS AND I WILL LOVE YOU ALWAYS

FOR SOMMER BROWNING

let's sit on this bench for
24 hours not telling
them where we are
you can gum up the engine while
I look for more time in my bag
there will never be another
golden age you say
WHAT A RELIEF I say
you smile finally
olfactory nerve slowly bent one way
then another by the rose
give me this planet as a friend and
I will show you how we have always
been wrong to fear
fire earth air and water
giants have come and gone and now
there are translucent salamanders
arms held out where
our friends can hear us
we loosen in this hour
we herald a breaking

calm appealing to
all muscle carrying
itself toward
and away until
there is no
center and not four
directions
but the
infinite
way
out

MY ELEGIAC SOMERSAULT WITH

YOUR PICTURE IN POCKET

the great apes are
my favorite cousins
I won't visit because
I don't endorse cages
sellout tourism of jails some call
zoos where no prisoner has
ever seen a lawyer
I have no idea how to free my cousins without
going to jail myself
what exactly are their crimes
it's never been clear on
these ulcerated days
maybe I should visit
give them comfort
these are my cousins
it's visiting hours at jail
why are these fucking
children here with cotton candy
take them to gawk at
drug dealers in human jail
you're sick and mean laughing at
my cousins
fire and water live together in
the sky
their sky names are
lightning and rain
when you die

whether human or ape
80 percent of you evaporates
joins raindrop congregations
the rest of you gets struck by
lightning over and
over until you are free

SHADOW OF GOLDEN EAGLE

PASSED THROUGH ME TODAY

hold me down in the casket
is what they will have to do
we abated our duel at dawn
eager to plant zinnias instead
digital zeros and ones talk into frosted fields
sentences milled to
perfect notions
a wish for the
canonized tongue a wish
that goes on and on
someone holds
me up to the boughs
forcing no utterance
letting ceremony escort
our oinks of affection
our carnival ride jacking *up up UP UP*
you would not read this poem if
you were first required to
swallow a feather
we can no longer
visit her house without
time travel
our ears are to
blame not words
all inference
resolved in the gut for
accumulated faces of the wind

giant black shadow coming
in across green fields
WHOOSH it passed through me
reuniting fragments to
wave the revival on

WONDERING ABOUT OUR DEMISE WHILE
DRIVING TO DISNEYLAND WITH ABANDON

don't be
afraid of
all we have pending
plasma I sold
in Albuquerque
broke even with
food I purchased to produce it
we can manage we can start under
this tree a quiet hour of
dozing into the bark will
reveal the step forward
things thinking about each other
this crystal and feather
ask me to bring them
together put them behind
the books they want a
private conversation and
that means me getting lost to
fellowship with grass soil and little
stones who tell me there is no clear
sense of when we leave this world
an owl drops a mouse in front of me
it doesn't have to mean something
but it probably does
help fishing a glass eye out of
the garbage disposal was my
favorite time helping anyone

he was so happy pushing it
back into his head shaking
my hand at the same time
we both wished he wasn't
my boyfriend's brother

LAUGH INTO SOIL

THEN SOW SEEDS

he puts it
down in
front of
himself
instead of passing it
this is the way of
men all over
the world
a camera with a pen wrote this poem
bending back into giant sleep
ink on pillowcase
night leaks into
mind's library
things you won't be able to
open without a
gun would include
my dreambank
we promised to
shake one
another into
a new phase
every few years
I sewed this heckler-proof
suit for you sorry you get
so much shit onstage
Clyde Barrow you
faggot bank robber

in my dream every bullet flew
back into their little piggy guns
were you ever so
strong as this
on earth

OUR PLANET TO THE HIGHEST BIDDER
DON'T ASK FOR THE DEPOSIT BACK

act no different than you feel
act no different than you feel
some will step away
others will sigh with relief
always remember nonmoral is not amoral
before you enter make a plow of
your hand to
test the air
they stamp your wrist to let you in
here's my stamp now leave me alone
pressing forehead to
wall gets ears seeing better
don't mention the wasp nest
they'll come with poison to
kill every one of them
we'll make peace with the nest
cooperation we learn on our own
at school it's only football and other war games
magpies eating entrails missing a face
it's all one cake for worms in the end
winter overlays a
white map toward
any direction
the night the kite came in on
no wind with no string
it was talking because
it was a talking kite

I'm Bob Kaufman and
Eileen Myles sent me
and he spoke no more
but hugged me
lots of hugs

THE ATAVISTIC QUALITY
OF YOUR EVERY CELL

through the
veil my limerence for
Elvis is reciprocated in
ways most would
not understand
keep the undies on
keep the music playing
we need a doorframe to
wedge ourselves for
what's happening next
it's not dreams it's
not dreams I repeat
I shot from His shaft not
in dreams a pool of His semen
how I came into the Memphis of everywhere
a sudden apport in Graceland
you in your bowling shoes
looking for me in the
dark rainy sky as if I
were flying home with
jackal breath over
my shoulder
shit stench sends
flies pulsing by the sink
a cradle of excrement we
made for years
attracting around

us a slow-burning
position in the dream
where imposters stay
angry to detract
from their masks

ISOTHERM PINPOINTS OUR
MUTUAL TRANSUDATION

fondle its
leaf before
chopping
it down
quiet things
assumed broken
each of us
pocketing manna from their veins
jack on don't jack off
what does that mean you ask
I show by example
quaking gender of
my splitting rib
you said your
urine was delicious
I didn't believe you
but now I know
you were right
into mouth jam this
light
into ceiling light of
the tongue
paint me with
your semen
ovate face
releasing
ovate thoughts to

shape your attention
keeping time with
dying oceans we
snort opiates for
fitting a floor to
our step

NAIL IT LIKE THIS AND YOU WILL
ALWAYS FALL OUT OF THE BLACK SKY

what exactly
would a
butterfly
require at
a butterfly toll
they will the calm on one another
get pushed into the meat sign
I saw 7 shooting stars tonight
made the same wish on each of them
something's got to come of it
tug mustard of the application
give them a price for
the blood I will
extract on the
spot if asked
he is always granted
access to the places
I am squeamish
ready to bite down
in his breast pocket the note I wrote
he hasn't found it yet
    he's at work
    he'll be by the
    river soon eating lunch
    he'll drive through tunnels pull off exits
    find it after parking outside the
    hardware store

asks himself if I mean it
assures himself the
flight down from
the stars is the way we
can get it all loved

DEVIL KEEPS A SOFTER
GRIP ON OUR CHEDDAR

enough shards of
light to wheel it
sunward
if you asked me to fight for
the color blue I don't remember
just stop yelling *blue*
blue BLUE
purple's fine
go with purple
average sensations on
an average planet as
long as people
fear their powers
for instance pine needles are
soft until cotton comes around
something's always
wrong around here
too much fighting
we don't love one another anymore
can't we burn a lock of
one another's hair and quit
   if you wilt in the dark
   I'll break your window to
   recharge your shine
   the singer stopped
   not by choice
   the song just left him

I put it in a cracker
asked him to eat until
increase of the
room came to our
ears once more

NO MORE SONGS FOR
MY DIRTY LITTLE WOW

sheer is my favorite
adjective a pleasure of
knowing something is certain
I don't need the photos I don't
know where they are anyway
jargonized by a leaf of quaking aspen
because *hello* is not the
correct working exclamation sheer agony
sheer silk
a motion to strike
anger out of the house
let's just make the word for
the day something that won't
tear away the sleep we need
it's going to cost a lot to
feel alive again
please understand a
crater in my
dream is none
of your business
you hold the
anchor in such a way
you won't fall
into motion again
you knew it was
over when we
gathered with fists of

flowers there was
no place else to
visit but the grave
and it was a shame you
wanted more

POEM AS SCONCE
FOR SOME LIGHT

it's not
impressive
your stiff upper lip
taking it like a trooper
do you need permission to
scream throw yourself into
the sofa sobbing
then I give it and
after that
the comfort
you need is something
I also offer for
I would never
do to you
what I have
done to myself
we burst out laughing
Eddie hanging by his
neck in a wedding gown
we felt awful I still do
but death can be
hilarious in the
wrench of not being
strong enough to keep
it away
swat it

death keep away from Eddie
oops too late
now what the
fuck am I
supposed to do

HOW THE FUCK DO I GET
OUT OF THIS PLACE

no I cannot win a knife fight
for the fifteenth time
I didn't see who
stabbed him
this line of
questioning
is exhausting
a truck has been
falling for forty years
no one can stop it
the driver long since
starved to death
we collaborate when
injuring ourselves
earache could be
from hearing
your last words
over and over in dreams
doctor says *it's mental*
I say *physical*
the ear can
only withstand
so many
whispers from the dead
you know as
well as I do to
hear this speech

pattern in the
wilderness is to
jostle us out of
forgiveness it
just cuts
us loose

MY ORGONE BOX OF GLASS BOTTLES

PILLOWS AND MUSIC

hi it's me don't listen to them I didn't die

join me upright at

the singe marks where

the cremation didn't take

I hate coffee but I just survived so

let me have some tossed high in

the branches of the miracle

middle age could be 25

you just don't know

only love can

interrupt the

waiting

someone culled a file of people looking for you

don't be such a coward our research proves

you're a perfect match

pull muscle layer over skeleton

then skin

all the hearts are defective

it's a punishing road of sorrow

label says *try not to wilt in the sun*

each of us has gunpowder in a secret organ

my therapist says *learn to live with it*

I say *learn to fucking eradicate it*

my clairaudient friend these

ghosts are here for your ears

at this very moment

there are 54 million

people on Earth who
will die over the next
12 months
some of them
tonight
be careful out there

TIME TRAVEL APPLICATION

FOR THE TROLL THREAD COLLECTIVE

I was invited to give a poetry reading in Buffalo, New York, April 7th. This is a time when spring is in FULL BLOOM in Philadelphia, while the land in Buffalo is still asleep with winter 400 miles to the north. On the train I had a photograph of snowy treetops and another of a worm-stuffed robin with violets. Every ten minutes I would look out the window. While what I saw was spring, I would hold the picture of winter to the window, step hard on a piece of broken plastic placed in my shoe and say, "THIS IS DEAD!" At the midway the pictures were switched, and I pressed into my now bleeding foot to say, "THIS IS ALIVE!" Notes for the poem were taken all along the rail. Spring rolled back into winter, the only season America deserves.

SCHEDULED POISON

writing
this poem
while my
nation brings
other nations
to their knees
syringe extracts
radiance of
dandelion injected
into jaw moving in mirror moving bright
sounds salvaged and accounted for
abuse us to amethyst for the
wish you would die list
no names just
drawings of their houses
tree in the yard
just kidding about killing them
just kidding just
ascertaining a thought
about thinking against
those mothers
minimize window of solace as
drone does
drone pilot is a real pilot?
this poem's pilot gets in there
we order food by the foot
if this makes sense to the future
something was right
pie-eating contest to salvation

dying to tell you of sex through hole in
the American flag GLORY HOLED
I for one tire of Mick Jagger singing in
grocery stores he never visits
put him in every car whose radio ever
played his song even the blackened
smashed windshield one with
bit of tooth on rug
       talk of forgiveness
       sickens
       FUCK your valor

MINDING THIRST

FOR JAMIE TOWNSEND

Watch weather report for heavy rain. On the day before, drink NOTHING. No beverages of any kind. Eat no soup or broth. Eat only steamed vegetables with soft noodles or bread. Wait for rain. Set your alarm to wake in the middle of the night, and then sit by the window peering into the dark sky with binoculars. Think about your first memory of being thirsty. Take notes, go back to sleep.

Wait for rain. You are still not drinking the next day and you are very thirsty. When rain arrives sit by the window. Close your eyes, take your pulse, hear the rain, feel your blood. Imagine that the water you hear coming to earth will never touch your lips, can never quench the dryness that is your mouth. Were you ever so thirsty that you were in pain? Open your eyes, take notes.

Go out into the rain. Lie on the ground. Look into the sky through binoculars with your mouth open. Drink DIRECTLY from the air while watching the streaming drops fall onto the binocular lens. Open an umbrella and take notes to the beating of rain. You are a drought that is cured. You are a body sponging back your life. Shape your three sets of notes into one poem or three.

QUA THIRST

I was thirsty in
1976 on our way
to a bicentennial picnic
35 years later we
eat burritos
become sad
tears of the cook
got into the rice and beans
most afternoons weepy
priests eat here
mourning their cocks
my suggestion of
castration upsets
everyone who fails
to consider
my concerns

KNOLL THIRST

bread asks
body to hold its
measurement of worth
crane my
neck back and
forth on telephone
glance at suit of
cards for their
sharpened edges
skid marks of
fatal crash
visible for months
there it is
there it is
oh my god there it is LISTEN LISTEN
I'm getting a tattoo of
your face on my
ass to show
you every time
you say goodbye

NECRO THIRST

it's hurting
me get out of
      my house if you
don't hate death as
      much as I do
    fuck you and your
    smug Buddhist calm
      alchemy of thorns
    from kind intentions
    it's none of your
    business if I trick
the doorman into
      thinking I'm
      his wife he
wrote my name
in a heart as
though I didn't
      ask him to

RESTORATION FIBER SONG

Go back to where you grew up. Don't let anyone know you're coming if there's anyone to let know. I went back, and the most important thing is to not write a single line of memoir, no autobiographical writing whatsoever. RESISTANCE is in the making, true resistance of the self. Immerse yourself with all the ways you felt about the world when living back there. Take notes without taking down memories, especially if you were suicidal. Where were you when you first researched the least painful way to go, the way that leaves no mess behind? Where were you when you finally realized it was impossible to not leave a mess behind? Go there and write about anything but this place, and write about what it's like to write about anything but this place.

There is a taste from your childhood. Find it, the taste you know well, a kind of candy or cake from a store out there. Take it to the river. You were loneliest by the river once many years ago. Go be there again. Be alone with your delicious childhood treat and smell it for a very long time. Write and keep writing without acknowledging the cake. Now RE-FUSE to eat it, and throw it in the river!! Write about something you love drowning as you watch it rush away with the current. This feels horrible because it is. Happiness is the place you went to after leaving when you were old enough and brave enough to leave. Go home, to the home where you made yourself happiest, and leave this broken spirit behind, unsated, untasted, and completely unwritten.

LAND OF THE SAPLING A

MERETRICIOUS TITLE

I have lost the will to grieve and need to find it
back of your dream taller smarter more in love
                    always leaving the wrong
                    amount of noise in the jar
                    "we're safe now" you say
                    I did not intend to laugh
                    come wander from the
                    central node with me
                    allow our
                    lonely song ample suffocation
study texture of the plank while stepping out
see our insufferable decline as irrelevant to
                    faces a fractured planet has
                    erased
                    but still you
                    order another table
                    as though it's tables
                    between us and
                    not everything else
                    "I'm living for the
                    future now" you said
                    and that was sad
                    dream positioning itself in the mob
                    trying the braid before
                    it gives up the
                    wrong way
                    an order to it

like ending life
kill the mosquito the right way
unless it's meant to open on its own
just one weed grows here without our help
stand before the song pleading we arise again
a new signal exits my mouth
I let it make its way
I WON'T STOP IT
to not die in summer
let life go
keep going without a
great phantom

HEALING FOR A PEDOPHILE

FOR VANESSA PLACE

I first thought about HEALING FOR A PEDOPHILE when I was in the middle of an earlier (Soma)tic poetry ritual, RESTORATION FIBER SONG. With the RESTORATION piece I went back to where I grew up, fully immersed myself in my old environment, especially the most painful of memories, but NOT ONE word of memoir was to be written. That was an exercise in resistance.

HEALING FOR A PEDOPHILE is a healing for a pedophile. My stepfather is quite ill with lung and heart disease and may not last the year. I spent much of my youth making certain he was never alone in the house with my younger sister. I was given my first rifle when I was nine, and would sit in her bedroom at night with the loaded gun pointed at the locked door, my sister hiding in a closet. John would be drunk outside the door moaning, "Show me your pussy, c'mon let me smell your pussy!"

A year ago my sister confessed a new piece of the story. I had moved out as a teenager since he only seemed interested in her when she was very young. It felt okay leaving, knowing that she would also leave in a couple of years, and I kept in close contact with her. But my sister recently told me that once when she was sixteen our mother made her get out of a hot shower, wrap a towel around herself, and sit on John's knee in the living room. My mother sat nearby, smoking dope and drinking gin. My sister says he didn't touch her with his hands, and that she jumped up and yelled at them both when he began bouncing his knee into her wet body. They laughed, or maybe just he laughed, I'm too enraged to hear the story again, and I have been incapable of seeing my mother or her creepy husband ever since.

Also about a year ago I became certified in Reiki, an ancient practice of directing our inherent personal reservoirs of healing energy through our hands to help others as well as ourselves. I was trained not only to dispense Reiki on people in front of me but also to send it long-distance. This was the most miserable (Soma)tic, taking notes for the poems during these healing sessions: First I performed Reiki on myself, then sent it to my sister. Then I sent it to our stepfather. The first time I sent Reiki to him I had to run to the bathroom to vomit. I didn't want to send it. The truth is I didn't want him to feel better, but I did send it.

The last person I sent Reiki to is our mother. Until my sister's latest story I had been able to fool myself into believing that maybe our mother was so abused herself that she chose to not notice her husband's proclivity for desiring six-year-old vagina. Our mother I will forgive last, she who compromised our safety to bring a little order to a pathological disorder. My nights of sleepless anger need to stop. Sending Reiki to those who deserve it the least heals me in turn, and I can feel the building peace in and around me with each session.

PS: At my "Impermanence Is the Old Permanence" lecture at MoMA PS1 I read this. Someone from the audience was upset because they have family who pray for them: they said, "I DON'T WANT MY FAMILY PRAYING FOR ME!" One big difference is that I'm not telling my stepfather and mother I send them Reiki, I just send it. In other words Reiki is not a weapon, like saying "I'm praying for you." I'm not interested in using Reiki to make them feel small, and bad. If I want to do that I only have to point at them and say, "YOU are a pedophile and YOU are his accomplice!"

NOTHING GENTLE

WILL REMAIN

freeze frame before
dinosaur grabs him
story from a blind
dog's perspective is
the movie I'm
waiting to see
white man with
bible in hand is how
the unluckiest
stories begin
things are always worse than we
allow ourselves to realize
it's too much to admit
this planet is a nazi
you must kill to
survive you have
to strike them down
from lettuce to cows
villainous planet
freeze us burn us
melt the ice but
do get on with it
dropping sugar
just dropping it
everywhere in here
many more faces to
make vanish to keep

fueling the day fueling
the day fueling the day
Placenta Jr. tell them
whatever flavor you
want because I have
a gun and they
left theirs
at home

I LOVED EARTH YEARS AGO

I drew a map on you so I wouldn't get lost. —DOIREANN O'MALLEY

Dear Eileen, every night lately I dream about Mark, my boyfriend who renamed himself Earth back when he became an environmental and AIDS activist. I no longer call his death in Tennessee a murder, I call it an execution, executed for being queer!! It happened over a dozen years ago and few believed my story and the police told our mutual friends he killed himself. An execution not fit for police investigation, just another faggot punished for breaking God's laws in this good Christian nation. I will never apologize for my anger!! Delinquent Films is making a documentary about my new book and they questioned me about Earth. They also didn't believe me so they interviewed the sheriff who told them Earth was a suicide. THEN they talked with the coroner and HE corroborated every detail I've been saying for years. Earth was hogtied, gagged, tortured, covered in gasoline and burned to death. The coroner used the word *homicide* and said it's not possible this was a suicide.

I'm grateful *homicide* was said out loud, and that a film about my POEMS is the reason this investigation is FINALLY going to happen!! What does it take to get a faggot's execution investigated? POEMS!! The weight of poems has arrived!! I loved him so much, my gentle, sexy man, steward of flowers and worms. I'm going to be on a panel at the Ecopoetics conference in Berkeley with some of my favorite poets. I'm creating a (Soma)tic poetry exercise where I visit the places Earth and I loved. We had a garden plot in Philadelphia, but we also planted zinnias, marijuana, cucumber, kale, cowpeas, rosemary, lemon balm, and string beans along riverbanks and in overgrown, abandoned lots. The weight of poems is upon me, so I'm selling them for a little ruthless surrender. A decade is long enough to dream of revenge for a dead lover. For seven days I'll go to our favorite places for the poems. I'll also go on the internet to see what every ingredient I put into my body looked like when it was still growing. See fields of sesame plants while chewing their seeds, YES!!

He named himself Earth when planet extinction was clearest. He wanted to spend time in Tennessee and I warned him about country people. I was born and raised in rural Pennsylvania where everyone is proud of living in the country. I noticed at a young age that these PROUD COUNTRY people LOVE to poison, burn, shoot, and decapitate the natural world. Their pride is mostly invested in SUBDUING nature, always ready to prove who's Boss! It is difficult to tell them who they really are, like convincing my stupid father to STOP pouring ammonia and broken glass down the chipmunk holes. It is difficult to convince them of the harmless lives of tiny creatures who only need a few acorns and berries. I miss Earth. I loved him. I'm tired of being such a sad faggot but c'est la vie. His brutal execution is a mirror of every decision to pollute air, water, soil, lungs, hearts, communities of people, birds, fish, bears, stop, stop, STOP, STOP!! Are you hopeful we can stop in time? Let me write some poetry and try to calm down. Love you Eileen, and thanks for listening.

ARIANA REINES SHOWED ME THE WORLD'S FIRST GUIDEBOOK WAS A 12TH CENTURY PAMPHLET FOR PILGRIMS

this is my refrigerator I won on
an American game show
once in a while I find myself
looking forward instead of back
hearing all dreamers talk at
once sends me into
the lower organs
I type your
name on the computer
delete it type it again
different each time
before I met you my
favorite color was
green light
now I serve poetry to
serve you
now I am famished for peace
now I watch a 90-year-old movie to
witness dead people talking singing
riding horses *samsara*
SAMSARA SAMSARA
I've been walking the border of sleep to find you
dreaming around the circumference of
a hole in the ground
the bravest thing sometimes is

how the morning is greeted
fight for the money or
fight for the soul the saying goes
but another goal is to
fight for neither

    drip drip

    drip the

    soul of money

    the loneliness of staying

    too long in a

    gentrified

    neighborhood

    tension of real

    things that

    seem unreal

    a door left

    open in the

    skull as

    a way out as

    a tyranny to

    let flow through the

    wires in the wall

    half the mind half the

    morning kept a secret from

    the cooling engine of

    the dream

    there is no

    job harder than

    setting eyes in

    sockets to see right

    most of your friends called you a

    suicide my dear man

but I know the truth in
saying I will always
love you is a
currency worth
the length
of my
time
here
How to Ruin the Child is chapter one of
my new book *How to Ruin the Adult*

GENDER CONTINUUM

FOR ANNE WALDMAN (AKA OUTRIDER ANNE)

Every morning for seven days I gave my friend Elizabeth Kirwin treatments of reflexology and massage, and she in turn gave me craniosacral therapy. Each morning while on the table I would fix my mind to meditate on seven possible genders for my body, intersex intersecting day to day. Starting with the female skeleton, hormones, glands, and genitalia. OF COURSE START with woman against the fairytale of Adam and his magical life-giving rib!

Day seven was male, but days two through six were variations of our world. The aim of physical, political, and sociological outcomes were in constant flux days two through six. Margins were permitted to drop in meditation. Permission to drop margins is an exceptional space to offer yourself and others. The craniosacral therapy was straightening my spine, relaxing my muscles, and challenging my thoughts throughout the gender exploration. The craniosacral lifted my consciousness while I was in deliberate concentration on the sex of my body.

Each morning after our healing exchange I would take notes about my physical condition—how it was shifting, mending—and notes on my gender meditation. The notes took no specific course other than a personal demand to divulge all hidden words and needs breaking free through the experience. I am a woman. I am a man. I will be neither, or bits and parts of both with blood and imagination-flow on the increase. And that increase is a prodigious stream tempering the spirit, today, tomorrow, again, again against a wall. Up the wall. Over the wall. Away from the wall. The world as it could be (or a collective version of it) is always trying to bend the air around itself to be heard. The risks of the day are holding themselves out to us, yet we all know too well that the power structure is far ahead of us, the ambush of the ages. My notes from this exercise were plucked and shaped into a poem.

STARTING TO START HEALING

starting it is starting in me
I am starting to realize
I say
galaxy when I
mean OUR galaxy
the Milky Way galaxy
future people
PLEASE know many
of us did not want
these wars
the armor in use
is a solid
imagination
against a
bullet
ultrasound
genocide machine
aborting girls to
preempt
burning witches
starting it is starting to amass a serious
dreamscape
start starting now
start having extra
places for us to
begin being
master in home
memory of caves
blurry in the

sensate mission

in my past

life reading I saw

you then I felt you

then wondered if you

were sensing this too

I have started remembering

I am starting to remember

Atlantis and so

are you

RADAR REVERIES

KINGDOM OF THE COATIMUNDI

FOR MICHELLE TEA & ALI LIEBEGOTT

I guess I should've closed my eyes when you
drove me to the place where your horses run free
— PRINCE

In July 2012 I attended RADAR Lab writer's residency in Akumal, Quintana Roo, Mexico. For nine consecutive nights I prepared my crystal-infused-water dream therapy to help me remember my dreams. Each morning I would recall my dreams, then listen to a different PRINCE album in its entirety, DIRTY MIND, CONTROVERSY, PURPLE RAIN, etc., allowing the purple PRINCE landscape to reinvent the dreamscape. As soon as the album finished I would write for fifteen minutes, which was not so much a dream journal as it was a dream-lost-inside-PRINCE journal.

After breakfast I went down to the beach. Each morning from 9 a.m. to noon I would sit in the same place, one foot closer to the tide each morning. On the last day I sat directly in the tidal break with sturdy paper and a pen whose ink embeds into paper, a pen invented to prevent check fraud. PRINCE may wash my dreams away, but the ocean would not take my poems.

For a few minutes I would close my eyes to listen to the tide. Then I would suddenly open my umbrella and stare at one of its polka dots, each one a different color of the spectrum. After staring at one polka dot for five minutes I would suddenly look out at the beach, coral reef, and ocean. The polka dot's color would show itself in the hue of a broken shell, or be found in the bow of a distant ship. One morning my eyes landed on the white of the umbrella, which is all the space surrounding the polka dots. I decided to go with it. When I tore the umbrella aside I noticed FOR THE FIRST TIME tiny white crabs who made their homes at the wettest part of the sand, continuously washed by the tide. The study of the crabs consumed my morning. One day I looked up from writing to see, a few feet from my face, a hundred yellow butterflies fluttering in a line down the beach above the surf. The parade of beauty kept me in awe: giant sea turtles, iguanas, and magnificent seabirds. One day I placed my large Lemurian crystal in the sand under the surf. RADAR Lab's amazing chef Christina Frank sat with me to witness the little silver fish surround the crystal. They LOVED IT! They would ride the surf to the crystal, surround it and KISS IT, ride the tide out, then ride it back in and KISS IT AGAIN!

From 3 p.m. to 6 p.m. I would sit in the bathtub to write. My favorite childhood liquid was FRESCA! I thought it went out of business, but it just moved to Mexico! I drank FRESCA all day long at the residency, and used it for the bathtub meditation, drinking mouthfuls, letting the grapefruit bubbles roil in my mouth while turning the shower on. I would touch the falling water with the tips of my fingers, then I would swallow the FRESCA and turn the water off. I would meditate on arguments from the archive of my unforgiving brain. Arguments I had, and arguments by others. Once I heard my mother and sister shouting in another room. My mother yelled, "I SHOULD HAVE ABORTED YOU!" My sister yelled back, "GRANDMOM SHOULD HAVE ABORTED YOU AND WE WOULD ALL BE FREE FROM THIS GODDAMNED MESS!" My mother BURST into tears, my sister left the room with a smile. She saw me and said, "I TOLD HER!" I returned her smile and hugged her saying, "YES you did my dear!" The MOMENT we embraced THE RELIEF of our grandmom's imaginary abortion WASHED OVER US BOTH! We laughed from so much pain and nonsense for a rolling tide. The brain holds all of our disasters in little, decrepit files marked and mismarked and repeating their vomitus sick, and sometimes a little too quiet from too much damage. These notes became nine poems, my homage to my mother who was not aborted, and to her children who were also not aborted.

ACT LIKE A PAINTED HEART

NOT A PAINTING OF A HEART

nothing
beautiful
came again
there is no
thing worse
i have crawled
on my knees to
end its
dormancy
scalp as verb
everyone has
a favorite verb
but mores replace
mores replace mores
scalping your enemies makes
outstanding souvenirs
we elevated
a flower
or maybe
it lowered us
an extraordinary
effort to forgo
the souvenirs
soon enough we were told
never leave the kitchen
with this knife again
no matter who is
bullying you

ACT LIKE VARIOUS

LIQUIDS AFTER A COCKFIGHT

replete is not
a word a cockroach would use
but she is
often as
satisfied
one person
is killed by
gun a day in
philadelphia
a strange
relief when
on vacation
even still if
we were on
a desert island
i would kill
you and eat
you immediately
i would WIN
i would WIN
i would WIN
I WOULD WIN

ACT LIKE PALLBEARER

WITH SOFA CUSHION

he's straight
so i guess he's
not into
fat guys?
maybe he
hates my
poems but
my poems are
fucking awesome
is there more
death or semen
in my first book
i'm afraid to
calculate
fuck anyone who
hates my poems
"no-no" you
assure me
"he likes your
poems he's
just straight"
what a pigheaded
inflexible world

ACT LIKE ADMINISTERED BY
SYRINGE TO THE DYING

you ask if i'm
a man or a woman
you only
know how to talk
to men
to women
making me a
small wild room
i've intensely acutely
exceptionally and
then exceedingly
HA
HA
HA you say
now you don't
annoy me in the
morning the
afternoon or
evening i have an
annoyance-free home
it's all breaking up on the phone
no not the signal us us us US US
what else sails backwards
through my throat
but your name
coatimundi saunter
golden twilight
betting against the
wild surviving our efficiency

ACT LIKE FLOWER

PULLING HIS PETALS OUT

let me know if
you need anything
i'm here to serve you
and just so you know
we're having a
sale on our
newest model it's
very nice it's where
your hand gets
held through the
difficult currents
later the
small ones
seem bigger
but our test
results show that
everyone who
hangs in there
winds up
ajar of their
former top
secret
desires
so please
let me know if
you need anything

ACT LIKE PERFORATED AT
THROAT TO TEAR AND POUR

                                you reject
                        no flower earth
                                i am
                                your
                                servant
                                serve
                                only you
                                chefs in a
                                bidding war on
                                the corpse i mean
                                meat
                                beef
                                it's beef
                                restaurant quality
                                means you can't
                                have it
                                at home
                                cook all
                                you want
                                still never
                        as good (you're a mom not
                        a chef "*shut up*" you say)
                                as brilliant
                                as you want
                                your human

magnificence
can never
lay a
turtle
egg

ACT LIKE POLKA DOT ON
MINNIE MOUSE'S SKIRT

i am not a
family-friendly
faggot i tell
your children
about war
about their tedious future careers
all the taxes bankrolling a
racist tyrannical military
i'm the faggot at
dinner asking to
be alone
with the
children
tell them their
future happiness
depends entirely
on how well they
cultivate rebellion against
any structure that
does not hold their
autonomy and
creative intelligence as a priority
CHILDREN your bliss is at stake
CHILDREN listen carefully for the
lies your parents tell you
CHILDREN prepare for joy in ways
none of them will ever imagine
prepare to live with no regrets

ACT LIKE EYE OF HORUS
TATTOO ON DEAD SWIMMER
ENTERING CREMATORIUM

call me downstage
to motion like the
photograph "it's a
photo" i say
"move like the
photo" they say
"but photos don't move"
they push a button under
a rock
suddenly every
photo on earth
moves for a
few seconds
calling me back to the
winter in
the story
cold bond
we grafted to
our longitude
belies our
latitude warm with sacrifice
trauma amped in
the evolution
another noontime angel told me a
room filled with people healing one
another
is what i must find

ACT LIKE HEAD LOUSE

BATHED IN SUNSHINE

                    i have been writing a war poem
                    every morning for
                    six years
(i have not cut my hair in
six years i wake to meditate on
how many war dead for every
inch of hair i hate the whole
fucking human race in
the morning i wake
dreading our
murderous
applications
of democracy)
                    all i
                    want is
                    to write a
                    love poem but
                    i am american and
                    everyone except other
                    americans understands
                    this futile dream
                    i want to burn
                    my war poem
                    cut my war
                    hair burn my
                    war hair burn these
                    words between

us i want to hold another
american's hand
in baghdad or kabul
and ask
only then
what love we could
possibly deserve

CATHETER ENJAMBMENT

FOR BRADLEY MANNING & MATTILDA BERNSTEIN SYCAMORE

And our lips are not our lips. But are the lips of heads of poets.
And should shout revolution.

— JACK SPICER

Let's be honest about our culture and say that anyone who makes us remember we are naked animals under these clothes is dangerous. To remove the scandal of it would first require the total annihilation of every bureaucratic agency sending memos through our doors. It is 2012 and some of us have our boots holding back the Return to Modesty campaign. The American homosexual in 2012 unapologetically celebrates surrendering to the dominant culture's taste for marital equilibrium and WAR! A swift, unmitigated return to values acts like bookends many willingly throw themselves between. The opportunity to challenge these stifling, life-threatening institutions passes out of the conversation entirely in 2012.

Stupid faggots putting rainbow stickers on machine guns! I'm going to say it: GAY AND LESBIAN AMERICA HAS STOCKHOLM SYNDROME! The campaign to be included in the multibillion-dollar military-industrial complex comes at a time when three children die of war-related injuries EVERY SINGLE DAY in Afghanistan. And after ten years of American occupation, Afghanistan has been deemed THE MOST DANGEROUS nation on our planet for women. No other place on Earth is worse for women than Afghanistan. How else can I repeat this so you hear it? America DESTROYS Afghan women and children! Did you hear it that time?

The genocide of thousands of gay men in Baghdad is a direct result of the American invasion and occupation of Iraq. The most famous homosexual apologist for fascism, Dan Choi, helped make this genocide possible while serving as an American soldier in Iraq. American gay rights are all that matter I guess? And the destruction of Iraqi gays is just another item on the list of collateral damage? WILL NOT SERVE! To be repeated, WILL NOT SERVE WILL NOT SERVE I WILL NOT SERVE! WILL NOT! Today I WILL LISTEN to only my voice for NOT serving this sanctioned, collective, and REAL evil.

In the morning I performed Reiki on a long, thin piece of plastic tubing, Reiki with intentions to BE conscious throughout the day of being queer. Queer. Only queer. Today I will NOT ALLOW anyone to change the subject when I talk about what it means to be queer. Today I will NOT ALLOW the liars to step in front of me. Today I will talk about the frustration of watching war go unquestioned by the homosexual community of America. Reiki. I did Reiki for half an hour on this plastic tube, then lubricated every inch of it, then inserted it inside my penis. It was not for pleasure of pain, it was for a chronic reminder of HOW this culture inserts its will on my penis more and more each day. You may now be married under our rules. You may now engage in the murder of innocent lives by our rules. I had many strained, bizarre conversations this day, constantly FEELING the tube inside my penis while walking around Philadelphia, while walking around Occupy Philadelphia and talking about war, genocide, and oil. The following poem is the result of this exercise, which was more painful in spirit than was the tube inside me.

IT'S TOO LATE
FOR CAREFUL

melting glaciers
frighten me when
appearing on
my street as
downpours
a feeling I send
ahead of myself to one
day walk inside
people sleep while I inspect their
flowers
not as
weird as
you think
I dreamt gays were
allowed in the military
isn't it great everyone said
what a nightmare I said
killing babies is less
threatening with a politically
correct militia
vices for the vice box
for
wards of the
forward state
who like different
things to kill alike

we CANNOT occupy Wall Street but
we CAN occupy Kabul
massage our
anger with a heart chakra green
blessings soaked into bedsheets
there's a way of
looking into
time for a poem
send it into the future
your footprint has
grown small what is
wrong with your footing?

                    what kind of American
                        are you? just buy it or
                            steal it but shut up
                        this poem is terrific for
                            the economy
                            the rich have
                            always tasted
                            like chicken
                            I'm not a
                        cannibal because
                            they're not
                                my kind

we CANNOT occupy Philadelphia but
we CAN occupy Baghdad
we're the kind of poets
Plato exiled from the city limits
FUCK Plato that
paranoid faggot
Don't Ask, Don't Tell?

HOW ABOUT
Don't Kill and say whatever you WANT!!
for instance
when I adopt a cat
I will name him Genet
"Genet! GENET!" I practice
calling Genet
INTO my LIFE!
when you purchase
a car the factory's
pollution is
100% free
it's never easy
waking to this
bacteria and light
mucus and bone
a legacy of stardust
it is 98.6 degrees Fahrenheit inside all
humans
the freshly
murdered
their murderers
and the rest of
us between
my father lived to
see the fast-forward to
the cum shot
technology's
authentic
application
we CANNOT occupy Oakland but

the ghosts will occupy us
I will stay and
watch our
phoenix rise
I believe
in us

GRAVE A HOLE
AS DREAM A HOLE

FOR BRENNA LEE

Set a clear quartz crystal on a shallow bed of salt overnight. When you wake flush the salt down the toilet, the crystal is now clean and ready for you. Dig a hole in the backyard. Sit by the open hole with the crystal; speak to the crystal in your right hand, close to your lips, telling it you will bury it overnight. Tell it you will dig it up next morning, then take notes and go to bed. (This transgressive act, putting a crystal BACK into Earth, I mean imagine someone taking a bone from your FOOT or below your heart, then putting it back for the night!! Sick, but also quite beautiful to permit ourselves this.)

Wake and write down ANY DREAMS you had in the night. Unearth the crystal, hold it in your right hand again and ask, "What was it like down there? Was it comfortable, please say. Was it fearful, please say." Hold the crystal in your left hand and write as fast as you can WHATEVER comes to mind.

Next night hold the crystal in your right hand telling it you will both climb into the hole of your dreams together. Place the crystal under your pillow. Next morning write down ANY DREAMS you had, then ask the crystal the same questions you did after digging it out of the backyard. ADD ONE QUESTION by asking the crystal if she had any dreams, or if we were traveling together. For seven nights alternate burying it in the backyard and placing it under your pillow. Take notes, take MANY NOTES. The crystal will translate the way to the poem(s) with you.

OBLIVIOUS IMPERIALISM

IS THE WORST KIND

is *ho-bo*
short for
something
i just got
called one
someone
recently said
"HEY your nails
are beautiful but
the rest of your
outfit is just okay"
glamour is my
great love but is
too expensive and
too much work
my beautiful
glittered nails are
my HOMAGE to GLAMOUR
every time i hear an interview
with a fashion model talking
about HOW HARD her job is
walking up and down the runway
up and down
so much walking
i become very tired in my
vicarious glamour fatigue
and i must nap

everyone around
the world knows
america's real
fashion statement
is bullet holes
every single
day we
spray the
arab world
with bullets
sometimes in
the faces of
babies we
don't have
special
little
bullets
for the
baby
faces they
have to take
our adult-sized
bullets right in
the middle of
their little
crying baby
faces BLAM take
THAT BABY it's
american
fashion

Acknowledgments

Many thanks to the editors and publishers who first published these pages in the following magazines: *Apartment Poetry*, *The Atlas Review*, *BathHouse Journal*, *Bombay Gin*, *Boston Review*, *boulderpavement*, *Broken Toujours*, *The Brooklyn Rail*, *Columbia Poetry Review*, *Conduit*, *Denver Quarterly*, *DREAMBOAT*, *Dusie*, *Everyday Genius*, *Gazette le Duc*, *Horse Less Review*, *jubilat*, *Matter*, *oote oote*, *NO INFINITE: A Journal of Poetry*, *PEN America*, *Phoenix in the Jacuzzi*, *Poetry*, *P-Queue*, *Salt Hill*, *Similar Peaks*, *small po[r]tions*, *The Toronto Quarterly*, *The Volta*.

Several of these poems appeared as part of *Poetry* magazine's podcast on The Poetry Foundation website, hosted by editors Don Share and Lindsay Garbutt.

Many thanks to the editors and publishers of the following chapbooks where some of these pages appeared:

Full Moon Hawk Application (Assless Chaps Press, 2014)
Act Like Polka Dot On Minnie Mouse's Skirt (Albion Press, 2013)
ECODEVIANCE (88 Press, 2013)
Translucent Salamander (Troll Thread Press, 2013)

Many thanks to the editors and publishers of the following anthologies where some of these pages appeared:

Best American Poetry 2014, edited by Terrance Hayes
and David Lehman (Scribner, 2014)

Best American Experimental Writing 2014,
Series editors Seth Abramson and Jesse Damiani (Omnidawn, 2014)

Some pigeons are more equal than others,
Editor Eric Ellingsen (Walther Koenig, 2014)

Privacy Policy: The Anthology of Surveillance Poetics,
edited by Andrew Ridker (Black Ocean, 2014)

Toward. Some. Air., edited by Fred Wah
and Amy De'Ath (Banff Centre Press, 2014)

Troubling the Line: Trans and Genderqueer Poetry and Poetics,
edited by TC Tolbert and Tim Trace Peterson (Nightboat Books, 2013)

Open the Door: How To Excite Young People About Poetry, edited by
Dorothea Lasky, Dominic Luxford, Jesse Nathan (McSweeney's, 2013)

*Kindergarde: Avant-garde Poems, Plays, Stories, and Songs for
Children*, edited by Dana Teen Lomax (Black Radish Books, 2013)

Gay City Anthology, volume 5: Ghosts in Gaslight, Monsters in Steam,
edited by Evan Peterson (Minor Arcana Press, 2013)

The Sonnets: Translating and Rewriting Shakespeare,
edited by Paul Legault, Sharmila Cohen (Nightboat Books, 2012)

*The Unexpected Guest: Art, Writing and Thinking on
Hospitality*, edited by Kenny Goldsmith, Sally Tallant,
Paul Domela (Art / Books Publishing, Liverpool Biennial, 2012)

Occupy Wall Street Poetry Anthology,
edited by Stephen Boyer (Occupy Wall Street, 2012)

Many thanks to the following foundations and
residencies without whom this book would not exist:

MacDowell Colony Fellowship, New Hampshire, 2013

Banff Centre Fellowship, Alberta, Canada, 2013

Machine Project, Los Angeles, 2012 and 2013: Poet-in-residence

RADAR Lab, Akumel, Quintana Roo, Mexico, 2012

Ucross Foundation, Clearmont, Wyoming, 2012

Pew Fellowship in Arts for Literature, 2011

Many thanks to Daron Mueller for publishing some of these poems in the
Ekphrasis, Visual Rhythm exhibition at the Boulder Museum of Contemporary Art.